PIANO EDITION
BOOK ONE

Band Expressions

Band Expressions Author Team

Co-Lead Author: Robert W. Smith

Co-Lead Author: Susan L. Smith

Michael Story   Garland E. Markham   Richard C. Crain

Contributor: Linda J. Gammon

Percussion Contributor: James Ca

Art Credits: page 5, *Butterfly II* by Paul Giovanopoulos, ©1995 Paul G
page 34, *Scenes of Daily Life in Korea* by Kim Junkeun, ©(
page 38, *Celebration 1975* by Charles Searles, ©Smithsonian American Art M....., ...g.... D.C./Art Resource, NY.

Warner Bros. Publications • 15800 NW 48th Avenue • Miami, FL 33014

Creative Tools of Music (Units 2 and 3)

Articulation—a slight interruption of the air stream with the tongue

Bar Line—a vertical line placed on a staff to divide music into measures

Breath Mark—a recommended place to breathe

Clef—placed at the beginning of the staff to identify the note names

Embouchure—the natural formation of the facial and lip muscles on the mouthpiece or reed

Fermata—hold the note or rest longer than note value

Final Bar Line—indicates the end of a piece of music

Flat—lowers the pitch of a note one half step

Grand Staff—treble and bass clef staves joined together

Interval—the distance between two pitches

Ledger Lines—short lines placed above or below the staff

Measure—the space between two bar lines to form a grouping of beats

Musical Alphabet—the letter names of the notes used in music

Rhythm—the organization of sound and silence in time

Sharp—raises the pitch of a note one half step

Staff—5 lines and 4 spaces on which notes are placed

Time Signature—a symbol placed at the beginning of the staff indicating the number of beats per measure and what kind of note gets one beat

4/4 4 beats per measure
quarter note recieves one beat

Musical Alphabet Games

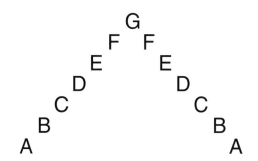
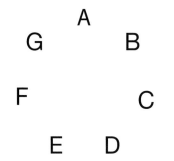

Air Stream

Inhale   E   x   h   a   l   e   Inhale
(1 2 3 4)   (1   2   3   4)   (1 2 3 4)

Band @ Home

LESSON 1

1. Teach one or more of your family members how to inhale and exhale in order to play a wind instrument.
2. Time how long you and your family members can exhale against a piece of paper.

LESSON 3

1. Create a variety of rhythms to sing with the recording of "One Note Rock" using the syllable "toh" or "doh." CD :4

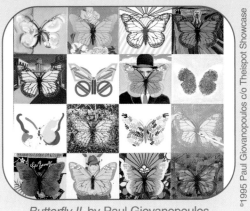

Butterfly II, by Paul Giovanopoulos

©1995 Paul Giovanopoulos c/o Theispot Showcase

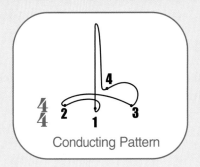

$\frac{4}{4}$

Conducting Pattern

1 *First Sounds*

Set 1　Ready 2　Breathe (3　4)　F

2 *Mouthpiece Rock*

CD :5

Play two times

Set 1　Ready 2　Breathe (3　4)　F → 　Rest　F → 　Rest

1 2 3 4 1 2 (3 4) 1 2 3 4 1 2 (3 4)

3 *First Note*

CD :6

Set 1　Ready 2　Breathe (3　4)　F

4 *One Note Shout*

CD :7

Play two times

Set 1　Ready 2　Breathe (3　4)　F → 　Rest　F → 　Rest

1 2 3 4　1 2 (3 4)　1 2 3 4　1 2 (3 4)

5 *One Note Reggae*

CD :8

Set 1　Ready 2　Breathe (3　4)

F → 　F → F → 　F F F F　Rest → 　go to next line

1　2　3　4　1　2　3　4　1　2　3　4　1　2　3　4

F → 　F F F F　F → F → F → 　Rest →

1　2　3　4　1　2　3　4　1　2　3　4　1　2　3　4

Band @ Home

LESSON 1

1. Practice "Mouthpiece Rock" with the recorded accompaniment.

2. Perform "Mouthpiece Rock" with the accompaniment track for your family.

LESSON 2

1. Perform "One Note Shout" with the accompaniment track for your family and/or friends.

LESSON 3

1. Practice playing "One Note Reggae." Practice your "toe-tap" with a steady beat while playing the quarter notes.

2. Show your family and/or friends the graphic *Butterfly II* and explain the groupings of "4." Perform "One Note Reggae" for your family and/or friends and read *Butterfly II* as your music.

3. Create your own graphic that represents patterns of quarter notes and quarter rests.

Creative Tools of Music

Critique—an evaluation of the quality of a performance

 Fermata—hold the note (or rest) longer than the note value

Intonation—the accuracy of pitch or pitch relationships in the performance of music

Ledger Lines—short lines placed above or below the staff for pitches beyond the range of the staff

Rest—a silent unit of time.

Soli—a line of music played by a small group of instruments

Tutti—all play

- Light blue highlights indicate new notes.
- Light yellow highlights indicate new rhythms.
- Light red highlights indicate new terms and symbols.

$\dfrac{4}{4}$ = 4 beats in a measure

Quarter note gets one beat

Quarter note = ♩ = 1 beat

Quarter rest = ↯ = 1 beat

6 *Learning Our First Note*

7 *Quarter Note Rock*

8 Fermata Warm-Up CD :10

9 More Quarters CD :11

10 Soli Jam CD :12

11 *My Quarters*

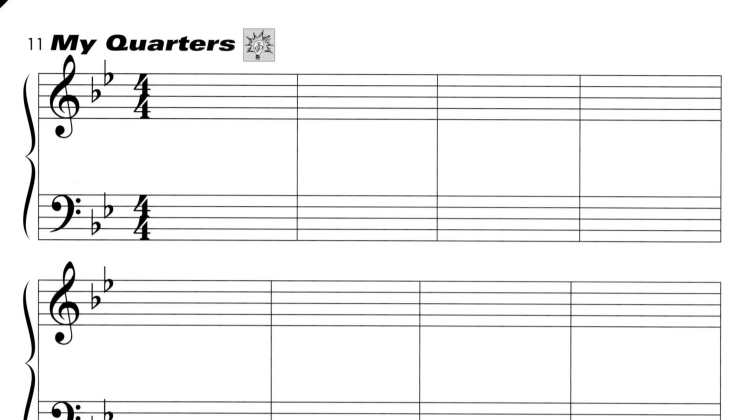

12 *New Notes*

13 **El Toro** CD :13

Band @ Home

LESSON 1

1. Practice "More Quarters" for our next lesson. This exercise will help you develop your music reading skills.

LESSON 2

1. Schedule a consistent, daily time for practice in a quiet place so you are not distracted and can focus entirely on your music.

2. Practice "New Notes."

3. Play "New Notes" for your family to show them what you have been learning.

4. Compose your own piece on the line entitled "My Quarters" in your book. Use any combination of quarter notes and quarter rests on your first note for the eight-measure composition. Be prepared to perform your composition in our next class.

LESSON 3

1. Practice "Mixing the Three" in Unit 5.

2. Explore www.band-expressions.com to find out more information about music and your instrument.

UNIT 5

Creative Tools of Music

Canon—a technique to compose music in which the melody is introduced in one voice and echoed by another voice

Solo—a performance by one person playing alone, with or without accompaniment

14 *Mixing the Three*

15 *Solo Rock* CD :14

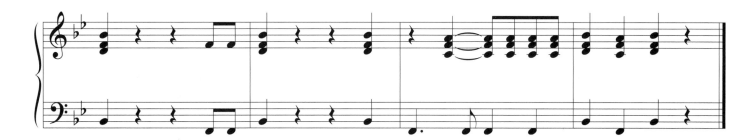

16 *Creative Expression*

17 *Going the Distance*

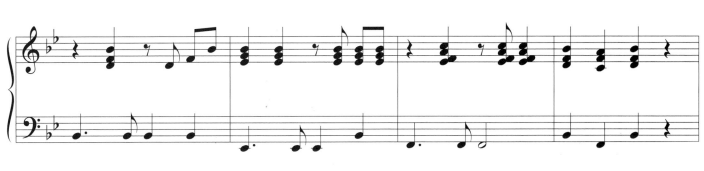

18 **Hymnsong** CD :15

19 *Putting It Together*

Solo   tutti

20 *Round and Round We Go*

21 *Canon Roll*

Creative Tools Notation

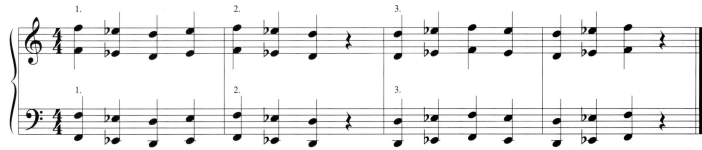

Band @ Home

LESSON 1

1. Remember—it is important to follow our daily practice routine.

2. Practice "Going the Distance." This challenging exercise reviews what we have already learned.

LESSON 2

1. Practice "Putting it Together." This selection reviews what we have learned to this point.

2. Remember the importance of the daily practice routine to build endurance.

LESSON 3

1. Compose and teach a family member a canon using body percussion.

2. Be prepared to teach your canon to the band in our next lesson.

3. On the "Creative Tools Notation" line, practice drawing your clef, time signature, barlines, quarter notes and rests, a fermata, and a final barline.

UNIT 6

Creative Tools of Music

Balance—all parts played and heard equally

Duet—a piece of music with two interacting parts

Harmony—the result of two or more tones sounded at the same time

Key—the tonality of a piece of music

Key Signature—flats or sharps placed at the beginning of the staff that indicate which notes are to be altered throughout the piece

March—music for a parade or procession

Musical Line—direction or shape of a musical thought or ideaa

Unison—all performers play the same note

Key of B♭

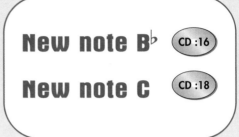

New note B♭ CD :16

New note C CD :18

22 *Three Note Warm-Up*

23 *Woodchopper's Ball* CD :17

Words and Music by
JOE BISHOP and WOODY HERMAN

unison

24 Two for the Show (Duet)

25 Two Tone Workout

26 Woodchopper's Ball CD :19
(C Version)

Words and Music by
JOE BISHOP and WOODY HERMAN

27 A "Rock" Nophobia (Duet)

(The Eentsy Weentsy Spider)

Traditional, U.S.A.

28 Heroes March (Duet)   CD :20

March

29 *Balance Our Sound (Duet)*

30 *Ode to Joy (Duet)* CD :21

LUDWIG VAN BEETHOVEN, Germany

Band @ Home

LESSON 1

1. Perform "Woodchopper's Ball" with the accompaniment CD for your family and friends.

LESSON 2

1 Play 'Heroes March' with the CD accompaniment for your family and friends.

LESSON 3

1. Perform "Ode to Joy" with the accompaniment track for your family and friends.

2. Explore www.band-expressions.com to discover more information about music and your instrument.

Creative Tools of Music

Chorale—a slow, "hymn-like" composition

Composer—a person who writes music

Phrase—a musical sentence or statement

 Repeat sign—symbol that indicates to go back and play the section of music again

PORTRAIT

John Williams

One of the most popular and successful American orchestral composers of the modern age, John Williams is the winner of five Academy Awards, 17 Grammys, three Golden Globes, and two Emmys. Mr. Williams has composed the music and served as music director for nearly eighty movies, including "Jaws;" "E.T.: The Extra-Terrestrial;" "Hook;" the "Indiana Jones;" trilogy and the "Star Wars" series. He is the Laureate Conductor of the Boston Pops Orchestra, which he conducted for 13 years and currently holds the title of Artist-in-Residence at Tanglewood, Massachusetts. He may be best known for the music he has written for the Olympics, including the well-known "Olympic Fanfare."

Whole note	= o	= 4 counts
Whole rest	= ▬	= 4 counts

Half note	= ♩	= 2 counts
Half rest	= ▬	= 2 counts

31 *Echo Warm-Up*

32 *Whole Lotta Fun*

33 Half the Time

34 Thanksgiving Song

Folk Song, England

35 Celebration CD :22

Words and Music by
RONALD BELL, CLAYDES SMITH, GEORGE BROWN,
JAMES TAYLOR, ROBERT MICKENS, EARL TOON,
DENNIS THOMAS, ROBERT BELL and EUMIR DEODATO

36 Whole Note Warm-Up

37 Phrase Phun

38 OK Chorale (Duet)

39 All Through the Night

Folk Song, Wales

40 Augie's Great Municipal Band (Duet)

 CD :23

Music by JOHN WILLIAMS

41 Theme From "Jaws"

Music by JOHN WILLIAMS

42 Creative Expression

Band @ Home

LESSON 1

1. Practice "Celebration" with the accompaniment.

LESSON 2

1. Practice the melodies we learned today.

LESSON 3

1. Practice the song "Jaws."

2. On line 42, compose your own shark song using the notes you have learned so far. Experiment with soft and loud and fast and slow to create different types of sharks. What type of shark are you?

3. Perform the shark song you create for your family and friends. You may have the opportunity to perform your song for the class in our next lesson.

4. Ask your family or friends to name a piece by John Williams. If they do not know any of his works, tell them about the music you heard or played in class. (Star Wars, Jaws, E.T., etc.)

5. Perform "Augie's Great Municipal Band" and "Jaws" for your family and friends.

UNIT 8 IS PRESENTED BY YOUR TEACHER

Creative Tools of Music

Anacrusis—one or more notes that occur as a lead-in to the first full measure

Dynamics—musical performace levels of loud and soft

Sight-reading—reading and performing a piece of music for the first time

Subdivide—dividing a note into smaller sections or fractions

Dynamic Markings

p	the symbol for piano, meaning to play soft
mp	the symbol for mezzo piano, meaning to play medium soft
mf	the symbol for mezzo forte, meaning to play medium loud
f	the symbol for forte, meaning to play loud

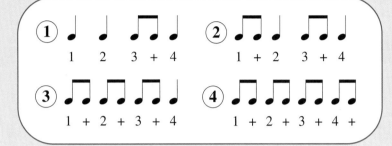

43 Playing the Phrase CD :24

44 Reading the Eighths

45 Three Pairs and a Caterpillar

46 Rain, Rain Go Away CD :25

Traditional

47 Creative Expression

48 Feel the Force! CD :26

49 Chitty, Chitty Bang Bang CD :27

Words and Music by
RICHARD M. SHERMAN and ROBERT B. SHERMAN

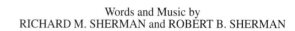

50 Arre, Mi Burrito! CD :28

Folk Song, Latin America

51 *Juba*

African-American Folk Song, U.S.A.

52 **Mary's New Groove** CD :29

Traditional, U.S.A.

53 **Duerme Pronto** CD :30

Folk Song, Spain

54 **Long Legged Sailor**

Traditional, Folk Song

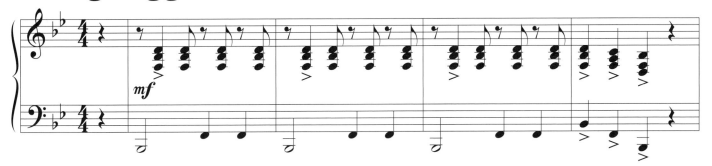

55 **Bang the Drum All Day** CD :31

(I Don't Want to Work)

Words and Music by TODD RUNDGREN

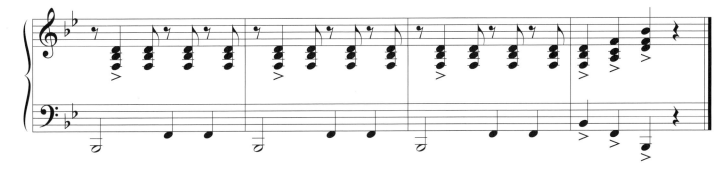

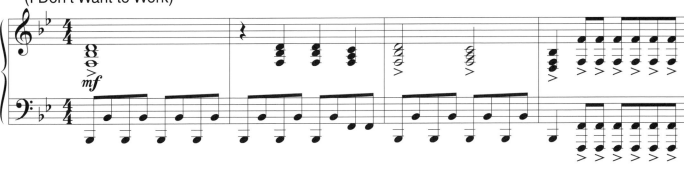

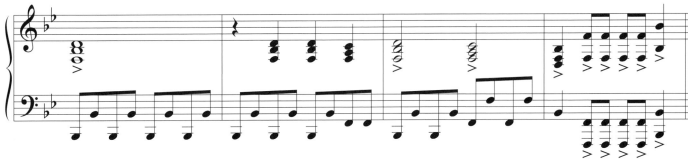

Band @ Home

LESSON 1

1. Play one of your favorite songs from earlier in the book.

2. On the Creative Expression line, create and notate four measures of eighth note and quarter note combinations using any pitch you can read and play. Clap, count, and play your composition.

3. Practice "Rain Rain, Go Away" with the CD accompaniment.

LESSON 2

1. Play the new song "Juba."

2. Draw dynamic symbols (piano, forte, mezzo forte, and mezzo piano) where you think they belong.

3. Play "Juba" with the dynamics you have added. Be prepared to play this in class next time.

4. Memorize "Rain, Rain Go Away."

LESSON 3

1. Teach the words to "Bang the Drum All Day" to your family and friends. Invite them to perform "Bang the Drum All Day" with you and the accompaniment track.

Creative Tools of Music

Melody—a series of musical tones that form a recognizable phrase

Ostinato—a repeated melodic or rhythmic pattern

Slur—a curved line placed above or below two or more notes to indicate that they are to be performed smooth and connected

Tempo—the speed of the beat

Tie—a curved line connecting two notes of the same pitch and played as if they were one

Tie   Slur

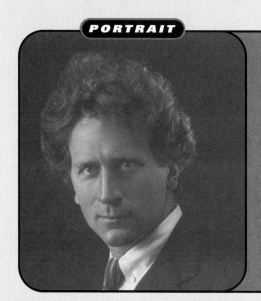

Percy Grainger
(1882–1961)

An Australian composer, he lived from 1882 to 1961. His music is based on folk songs he collected from throughout the British Isles. He used a phonograph to record men and women singing the songs that were passed down to them from their parents and grandparents. In his arrangements of these folk songs for band, he tried to keep the phrasing as close to the original vocal performance as possible.

56 *New Vistas*

57 Claire de Lune

Folk Song, France

58 Mary With My New Notes

Traditional, U.S.A.

59 Los Pollitos CD :33

Folk Song, Ecuador

Band Expressions

60 ***When the Saints Go Marching In***   CD :34

JAMES M. BLACK and
KATHERINE E. PURVIS, U.S.A.

61 ***Catch a Falling Star***   CD :35

Words and Music by
PAUL VANCE and LEE POCKRISS

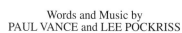

62 ***Sarasponda***

Folk Song, Holland

63 ***Shepherd's Hey*** CD :36

Country Dance, England

Band @ Home

LESSON 1

1. Complete "Mary With My New Notes" by notating the missing melody. We will play our completed song in our next lesson.

2. Practice playing "Claire De Lune" with the accompaniment track.

LESSON 2

1. Practice "Los Pollitos," "When the Saints Go Marching In," and "Catch a Falling Star" at different tempi.

2. Explain and play for someone at home the difference between a tie and a slur.

3. Revise "Mary With My New Notes" looking for:

   • Straight note flags
   • Neatly written note heads
   • Correct notes
   • Evenly spaced notes

4. Add the following to your composition:

   • New appropriate words
   • Dynamics

5. Be prepared to share your composition with the band.

LESSON 3

1. Create a one measure rhythmic ostinato to accompany "Mary With My New Notes".

2. Your ostinato should be on the note (F) using any combination of quarter and eighth notes and quarter rests.

3. Remember that an ostinato is a repeated pattern.

Creative Tools of Music

> **Accent**—play the note with more emphasis

Chord—three or more tones sounded at the same time

♩. **Dot**—increases the value of the preceding note or rest by one half

1st and 2nd Endings—play the first ending the first time only and the second ending the second time

3/4 **Time Signature**—a symbol placed at the beginning of the staff with the top number indicating that there are 3 beats per measure, and the bottom number indicating a quarter note, which equals one beat

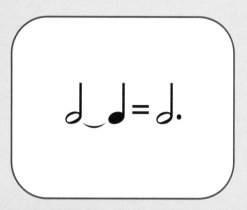

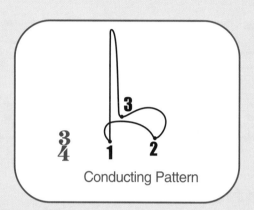

Conducting Pattern

PORTRAIT

Gustav Holst
(1874–1934)

Gustav Holst was born in Cheltenham, England in 1874 and began composing while at Cheltenham Grammar School. While studying at the Royal College of Music, he met Ralph Vaughan Williams, another famous composer, and the two were close friends, always playing drafts of their newest compositions to each other. Holst was a teacher his whole life and because of a heavy and demanding teaching load, it took him many years to write his most famous work, "The Planets" (1914-1916). Despite his initial training at the Royal College of Music, Holst was largely self-taught as a composer, mostly learning by experience. He was an intense nationalist, and after his rejection from the Royal military because of his bad eyesight, he became a conductor of the military band, and toured much of Europe supporting the British through music. Some of his most well-known pieces include "Moorside Suite," "Suite in E♭," "Suite in F," and "The Planets."

64 *Three at a Time*

65 Batman Theme

Words and Music by NEAL HEFTI

66 Around Her Neck

Traditional, U.S.A.

She Wore a Yellow Ribbon

67 **Shusti Fidli**

Folk Song, Czechoslovakia

68 **Change the Drum**

69 *Oh Dear, What Can the Matter Be?* CD :40

Folk Song, England/Scotland

70 *In the Bleak Midwinter* CD :41

GUSTAV HOLST, England

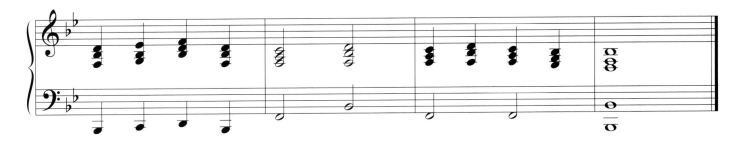

Band @ Home

LESSON 1

1. Practice "Batman Theme" and "Around Her Neck."
2. Perform these songs for your family and friends. You may wish to ask your family if they remember "Batman Theme" from the classic television series.

LESSON 2

1. Explain 3/4 time to one of your family members.
2. Ask them to count for you as you play "Shusti Fidli."
3. Practice conducting each exercise before performing.

LESSON 3

1. Create and notate a new 8-count accent pattern. Be prepared to notate the pattern on the board during our next lesson for the band to play.
2. Practice "Oh Dear, What Can the Matter Be?" and "In the Bleak Midwinter."
3. Teach one of your family members how to conduct in a 3/4 time signature. Ask the family member to conduct as you play "Oh Dear, What Can the Matter Be?"

Creative Tools of Music

Accidental—a sharp, flat or neutral, in a way not indicated in the key signatures

Concert pitch—the actual sounding pitch of a note played by an instrument

Introduction—a short section of music preceding the piece

Natural—this symbol cancels a previous sharp or flat sign; like a flat or sharp, it is used for the entire measure

Rock—a style of popular music that originated in America, characterized by a strong rhythmic beat and electronic instruments

Concert Pitch	F	D	E♭	B♭
C Instruments	F	D	E♭	B♭
B♭ Instruments	G	E	F	C
E♭ Instruments	D	B	C	G
F Instruments	C	A	B♭	F

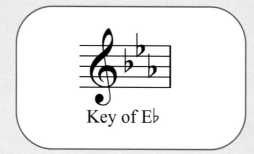

Key of E♭

71 *Song in E Flat*

72 *There's No One Exactly Like Me*

By BETTY ANN RAMSETH

73 *March Flam* CD :42

74 Happy Birthday to You!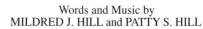

Words and Music by
MILDRED J. HILL and PATTY S. HILL

75 Jingle Bells   CD :44

J. PIERPONT, U.S.A.

76 Jingle Bell Rock   CD :45

Words and Music by JOE BEAL and JIM BOOTHE

77 **Sunrise, Sunset**

Lyrics by SHELDON HARNICK
Music by JERRY BOCK

78 **Hine Ma Tov** CD :47

Folk Song, Israel

Band @ Home

LESSON 1

1. Practice "There's No One Exactly Like Me" and "Happy Birthday to You!"

2. Perform "Happy Birthday to You!" for your family and friends.

LESSON 2

1. Practice "Jingle Bells" and "Jingle Bell Rock" alone and with the accompaniment tracks.

2. Memorize "Happy Birthday to You!"

LESSON 3

1. Practice playing the notes in your Concert Pitch Grid.

2. Practice playing concert pitches with a friend from band or while you play the concert pitches on the piano or keyboard.

UNITS 13–15

Creative Tools of Music

Balance—the dynamic strength and importance given to instruments/voices within a composition

Multiple Measure Rest—a symbol indicating more than one measure of rest

3 **Rehearsal Numbers/Letters**—markings above the staff that indicate specific locations in the music

Sight-reading—the playing of a piece of music for the first time

Style—how notes, rhythms, and articulations are treated in musical performance

SIGHT–READING PROCEDURE MAP (SRPM)

1. Look at the title, composer, time signature, and key signature.

2. Look through the entire piece for the musical road map and for any key or time signature changes.

3. Follow along each line of music with your finger to be sure you know all of the notes and understand all of the rhythms and musical markings.

4. Count through the entire piece silently while tapping your foot.

5. Finger/airstick through the entire piece. Be sure to look at the words and symbols around the notes for all of the performance information.

6. Silently practice the difficult passages.

---

79 **Lotta Latin**

80 ***Feliz Navidad*** 3 CD :48

Words and Music by JOSE FELICIANO
Arranged by MICHAEL STORY

81 **Up on the Housetop** CD :49

BENJAMIN RUSSELL HANBY, U.S.A.
Arranged by MICHAEL STORY

82 **Rock Warm-Up**

83 **Winter Wonderland** can be found on page 40.

84 **Holiday Warm-Up**

83 **Winter Wonderland**   CD :50

Words by DICK SMITH
Music by FELIX BERNARD
Arranged by ROBERT W. SMITH

83 **Holiday Warm-Up** can be found on pages 39.

85 **We Wish You a Merry Christmas**

Traditional, England
Arranged by ROBERT W. SMITH

86 **Dynamic Warm-Up**

87 **African Patapan** CD :51

Carol, France
Arranged by MICHAEL STORY

88 *Concert Chorale*

Band @ Home

UNIT 13

LESSON 1

1. Practice "Feliz Navidad."

LESSON 2

1. Practice "Feliz Navidad" and "Up on the Housetop," considering the style for each piece.

2. Remember to isolate the more difficult passages, playing them slowly and gradually increasing the speed.

3. Record yourself playing your part on "Feliz Navidad." Write down what you discovered from critically listening to yourself play.

Band @ Home

UNIT 14

LESSON 1

1. Review all three of the concert pieces, striving for individual improvement.

2. Make a recording of your performance of each piece and turn it in at our next lesson. Your teacher will review your recording and provide feedback for improvement.

LESSON 2

1. Review all of the concert pieces we have learned so far. If you are having difficulty with particular sections of a piece, play the section slowly to improve before going on.

Band @ Home

UNIT 15

LESSON 1

1. Review all of the concert pieces.

LESSON 2

1. Polish your performance on all of the concert pieces and prepare all music, equipment, and concert attire.

2. Tell your family and friends the reporting time and concert time.

UNITS 16—18 WILL BE PRESENTED BY YOUR TEACHER

UNIT 19

Creative Tools of Music

Allegro—fast tempo

Moderato—moderate or medium tempo

Andante—slow (walking) tempo

89 New Horizon Warm-Up

90 Finger Stretch

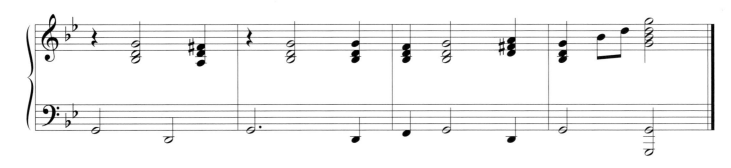

91 *Marianne* CD :52

Folk Song, Jamaica

92 **Scooby-Doo, Where Are You?** CD :53

Words and Music by
DAVID MOOK and BEN RALEIGH

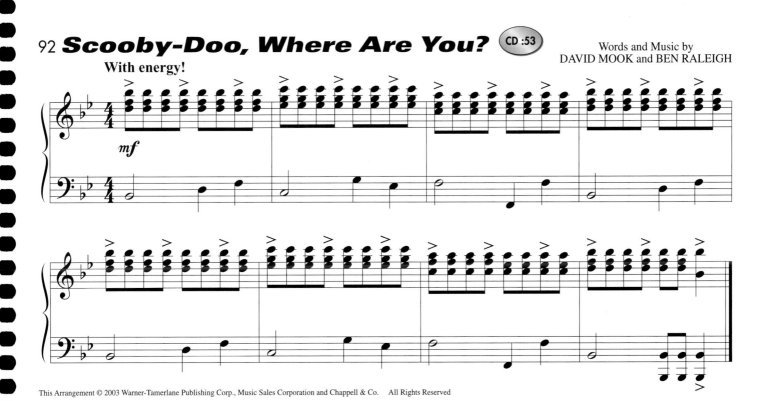

93 *Over There* CD :54

Words and Music by
GEORGE M. COHAN

94 **The Chicken Dance** CD :55
(a/k/a Dance Little Bird)

By TERRY RENDALL and WERNER THOMAS

95 **Walking Waltz**

Andante

96 Moderato March

97 Go, Go, Allegro!

98 Can Can

 CD :56   CD :57   CD :58

JACQUES OFFENBACH, France

Andante/Moderato/Allegro

99 Creative Expression

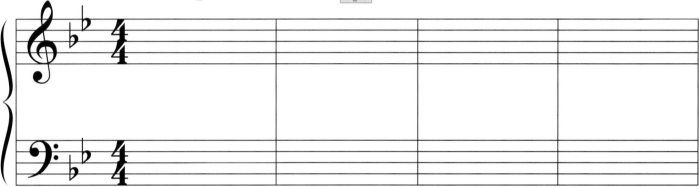

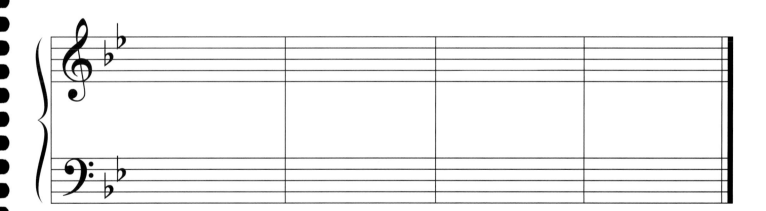

Band @ Home

LESSON 1

1. Practice "Marianne" and "Scooby Doo, Where Are You?" with the accompaniment CD.

2. Perform "Marianne" and "Scooby Doo, Where Are You?" for a family member or friend. Ask them if they have heard these songs before and if so where.

LESSON 2

1. Practice "Over There" and "The Chicken Dance."

2. Make up new appropriate motions to "The Chicken Dance" and teach them to someone in their family.

LESSON 3

1 Practice "Can Can" at Moderato, Allegro, and Andante tempi.

2. Explain the different tempi to one of your family members and perform "Can Can" at those tempi.

3. Create an 8-measure rhythmic composition on the staff provided and then apply the tempo markings you have learned in this lesson—Moderato, Allegro, and Andante. Perform your composition using a selected note.

PORTRAIT

Aaron Copland
(1900-1990)

Aaron Copland composed musical works for ballets, orchestras, choirs, and the movies. He composed "Billy the Kid" and "Rodeo," music based on American folklore. He also composed "Lincoln Portrait," which was a tribute to President Abraham Lincoln. One of Copland's best-known works is "Fanfare for the Common Man."

Key of F

100 *Siren Warm-Up*

101 *Great Granddad*

Cowboy Song, U.S.A.

102 **Git Along Little Dogies**

Cowboy Song, U.S.A.

103 Goodbye Old Paint

Cowboy Song, U.S.A.

104 Shaker Hymn

Appalachian Folk Song, U.S.A.

105 Five Foot Two, Eyes of Blue

Lyric by SAM LEWIS and JOE YOUNG
Music by RAY HENDERSON

Allegro

106 The Hey Song CD :59

By MIKE LEANDER and GARY GLITTER

Rock

11

107 New for a Few

108 Norwegian Mountain Dance

Folk Song, Norway

109 **The Merry Go Round Broke Down** CD :60

Words and Music by
CLIFF FRIEND and DAVE FRANKLIN

Allegro

110 **Creative Expression** *Complete the Composition Worksheet #13.*

Band @ Home

LESSON 1

1. Perform the three selections learned today, "Git Along Little Dogies," "Great Granddad," and "Goodbye Old Paint," for your family.

LESSON 2

1. Play "Shaker Hymn" for your family. Ask if they have heard this song before.

2. Tell your family that Aaron Copland used "Shaker Hymn" in his composition "Appalachian Spring."

3. Play "The Hey Song" with the accompaniment track.

LESSON 3

1. Perform, "Norwegian Dance", and "The Merry-Go-Round Broke Down" for your family and friends.

2. Complete Worksheet #13, "110 Creative Expression."

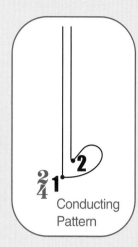

UNIT 21

Creative Tools of Music

Measure Repeat Sign— a symbol that indicates to repeat the previous measure

$\frac{2}{4}$ **Time Signature—** 2 beats per measure Quarter note receives one beat

Conducting Pattern

Mariachi Cobre

111 *Back to Home*

Andante

112 *Getting Even*

Moderato

113 *Cucu Cucu*

Folk Song, Spain

Allegro

mf

114 *Cielito Lindo* CD :61

Folk Song, Mexico

Allegro

f

115 *Building the Long Tone*

Moderato

116 *Eighth Rest Workout*

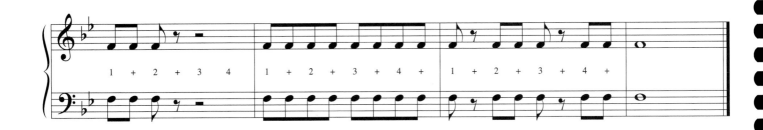

117 *Mi Caballo Blanco*

Folk Song, Chile

118 ***Rest on the Beat***

119 ***El Juego Chirimbolo*** CD :62

Folk Song, Ecuador

120 ***Relay Game***

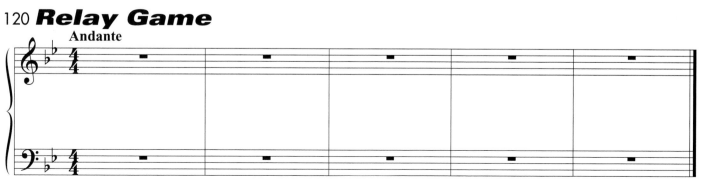

121 *San Sereni*

Folk Song, Latin America

122 *La Cucaracha*

Folk Song, Mexico

123 **El Relicario** CD :63

Moderato

Folk Song, Mexico

124 **Creative Expression**

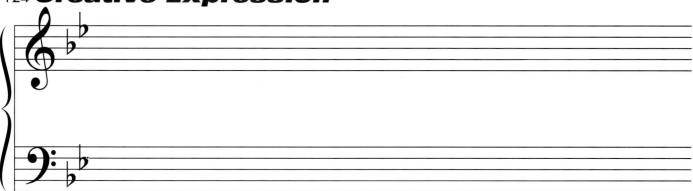

Band @ Home

LESSON 1

1. Play "Cielito Lindo" and "Cucu Cucu" for your family and friends.

LESSON 2

1. Practice "Eighth Rest Workout" and "Rest on the Beat."

2. Play "El Juego Chirimbolo" for your family and friends.

LESSON 3

1. Practice "San Sereni," "La Cucaracha," and "El Relicario."

2. On line 124 write a song using the following: 2/4 time signature, eighth notes and rest, repeat sign, and any of the pitches we have learned so far.

UNIT 22

Creative Tools of Music

Legato—smooth and connected without interruption between the notes (soft start, long duration)

Staccato—play the note lightly and detached (light start, short duration)

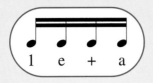

Tenuto—play full value (long duration)

125 Theme From "The Surprise Symphony"

FRANZ JOSEPH HAYDN, Austria

126 Song of the Volga Boatmen

Folk Song, Russia

127 **Paradiso** CD :65

By ROBERT W. SMITH

128 **Smooth Sailing**

129 Dance of the Reed Flutes

PETER ILYICH TCHAIKOVSKY, Russia

130 The Long and Short of It

131 Sea Chanty CD :66

Traditional Sea Chanty, England

132 Can Can

Moderato

JACQUES OFFENBACH, France

133 Wipe Out CD :67

Moderate rock

By THE SURFARIS

Band @ Home

LESSON 1

1. Practice staccato articulations on all of the songs you have learned today. It will take daily practice to train the muscles necessary to play articulations.

2. Practice the "Surprise Symphony" with the accompaniment.

LESSON 2

1. Practice staccato and legato articulations. Practice slowly and carefully using the exact method needed for each articulation style.

2. Sight-read "Sea Chanty" as an example of legato and staccato style.

LESSON 3

1. Practice playing staccato, legato, tenuto, and slurs. Improvise with each articulation style on any exercise we have played so far and decide which articulation sounds the best. It will take daily practice to develop the muscles necessary to produce these varying articulations and styles.

Creative Tools of Music

Scenes of Daily Life in Korea, by Kim Junkeun

19th Century, ©Christie's Images Ltd. 1996

Crescendo—gradually get louder.

Decrescendo—gradually get softer.

Largo—very slow tempo

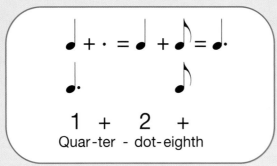

134 ***Louder and Softer***

Andante

135 ***Ouma*** CD :68

Mother Horse and Colt

Folk Song, Japan

Moderato

136 **Sakura**
Cherry Blossoms
Andante

Folk Song, Japan

137 **Kaeru No Uta (Duet)**

Folk Song, Japan

Moderato

138 **Pentatonic Warm-Up**

Moderato

139 Dots

140 Ha'kyo Jung

Folk Song, Korea

141 Hua Gu Ge

Folk Song, China

142 Arirang

Folk Song, Korea

143 Dotted Note Warm-Up

144 *Largo From "The New World Symphony"*

Largo

ANTONÌN DVORÀK, Czechoslovakia

145 *Crescent Moon*

Folk Song, China

Moderato

146 *Creative Expression* Compose a pentatonic melody and ryhthm accompaniment on Worksheet #16.

Band @ Home

LESSON 1

1. Practice the pieces we played today, working to improve the articulations and crescendo and decrescendo. Practice slowly and carefully, remembering to use the exact method needed for each articulation style.

LESSON 2

1. Practice the "Pentatonic Warm-up" and "Arirang." Make a recording of both of these for review. Feedback on your progress will be provided.

2. You will turn in your recording of "Arirang."

LESSON 3

1. Practice and perform your favorite pieces of Asian music we studied this week.

2. Complete Worksheet #16, 146 Creative Expression.

3. Practice your composition and be prepared to perform for the class.

Creative Tools of Music

Da Capo (D.C.)—return to the beginning

Fine—the end

PORTRAIT

George Gershwin
(1898–1937)

George Gershwin's songs are some of the most lasting modern popular music written in the 20th Century. George Gershwin died when he was still fairly young. He is credited with being one of the first composers to merge jazz and classical music styles. One of his most famous works is the folk opera "Porgy and Bess."

147 *Low Tone Warm-Up*

148 *Register Change Exercise*

149 Golden Gate March

Moderato

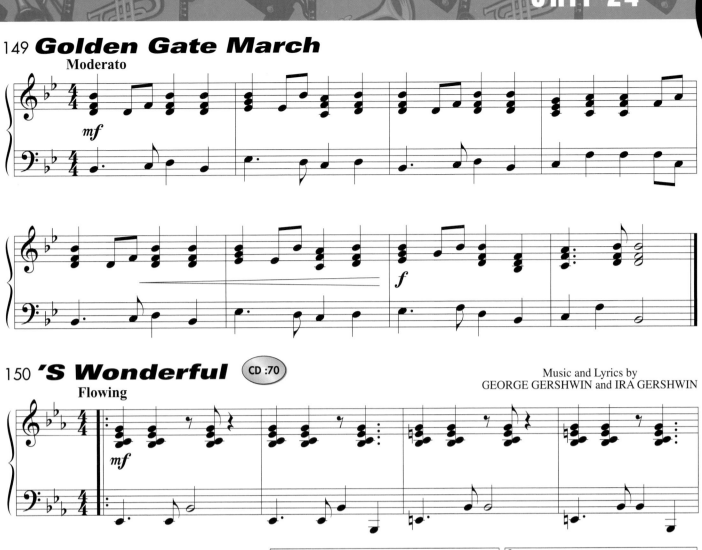

150 'S Wonderful

CD :70

Music and Lyrics by
GEORGE GERSHWIN and IRA GERSHWIN

Flowing

151 Rhapsody in Blue™

CD :71

By GEORGE GERSHWIN

Flowing

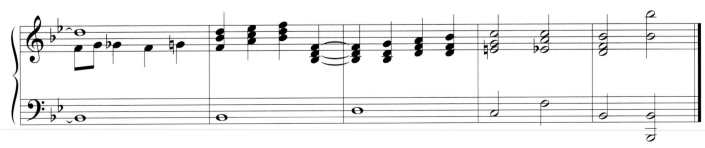

152 The Donkey Song

Traditional, U.S.A.

Fine   *D.C. al Fine*

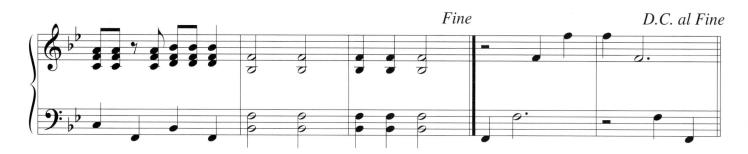

153 Summertime CD :72

Smoothly

By GEORGE GERSHWIN, DuBOSE and
DOROTHY HEYWARD and IRA GERSHWIN

154 **I Got Rhythm** CD :73

Music and Lyrics by
GEORGE GERSHWIN and IRA GERSHWIN

155 **Creative Expression/Arrange and Notate**
Arrange and notate on Worksheet #17.

Band @ Home

LESSON 1

1. Practice "Rhapsody in Blue" and "'S Wonderful."

LESSON 2

1. Practice "Summertime" and "Donkey Song."
2. Practice "Register Change Exercise."

LESSON 3

1. Practice "Summertime" and "I Got Rhythm" with the accompaniment tracks.
2. Complete Worksheet #17, 155 Creative Expression.

Creative Tools of Music

Drum Circle—an interactive group of people gathered in a circle to play music on percussion instruments; a facilitator who directs the group in rhythm activities and improvised patterns usually leads a drum circle

Ritardando (Rit.)—gradually slow down

Celebration, by Charles Searles (b. 1937)

Syncopation—rhythm with the emphasis or stress on a weak beat or weak portion of a beat

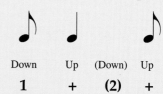

Down	Up	(Down)	Up
1	**+**	**(2)**	**+**

©Smithsonian American Art Museum, Washington, D.C., Art Resource, N.Y.

156 **You're a Grand Old Flag** CD :74

GEORGE M. COHAN, U.S.A.

157 **Hill and Gully** CD :75

Folk Song, Jamaica

158 **Cheki, Morena**

Folk Song, Puerto Rico

159 African Warm-Up
Marilli

160 Che Che Koolay CD :76

Singing Game, Ghana

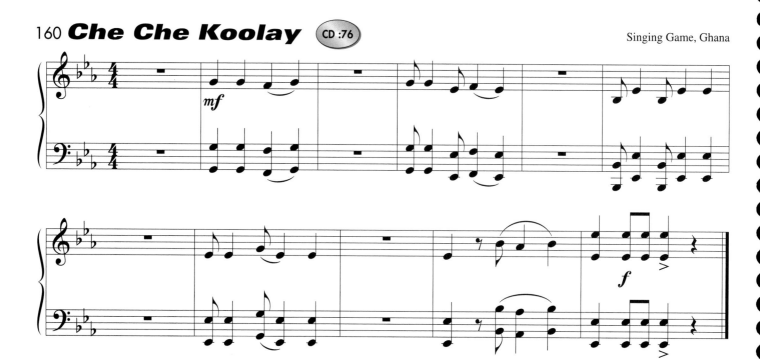

161 **The Rooster's Call**

Folk Song, Liberia

162 **Green Sally Up**

Folk Song, U.S.A.

163 Hello Lungile CD :77

Lively!

Folk Song, South Africa

164 Lil' Liza Jane

Words and Music by
COUNTESS ADA DELACHAU, U.S.A.

Dixieland

Band @ Home

LESSON 1

1. Practice "You're a Grand Old Flag" and "Hill and Gully" with and without the accompaniment tracks.

2. Create your own warm-up with syncopation and be prepared to share it with the band during our next class.

LESSON 2

1. Practice "Che Che Koolay" and "The Rooster's Call."

2. Describe a drum circle to several friends and/or family members and lead them in a drum circle performance. Find something resonant that sounds like a drum when played with your hands such as a box, can, or container.

LESSON 3

1. Practice "Green Sally Up" and "Hello Lungile."

UNIT 26

IS PRESENTED BY YOUR TEACHER

Creative Tools of Music

Jazz—music rooted in improvisation and characterized by syncopated rhythms

𝄋 **Dal Segno (D.S.)**—repeat from the sign

Improvisation—the process of spontaneously creating a new melody

Swing—a style of jazz music characterized by the "lengthening" of the eighth notes that are on the beat

PORTRAIT

Edward Kennedy "Duke" Ellington
(1899-1974)

Duke Ellington is remembered as one of the greatest jazz artists and important composers of the Twentieth Century. He wrote thousands of compositions, which included jazz music, sacred music for the church, show music, and music for movies. Mr. Ellington composed jazz classics such as "It Don't Mean a Thing (If it Ain't Got That Swing)" and "Satin Doll." He was also a brilliant conductor, arranger, pianist, and bandleader.

165 *Gentle Warm-Up*

166 *Chorale*

167 **Angel Band**

African-American Folk Song, U.S.A.

Gospel

168 **Duke's Place** CD :78

(a/k/a C Jam Blues)

Music by DUKE ELLINGTON
Lyrics by RUTH ROBERTS, BILL KATZ and ROBERT THIELE

Swing

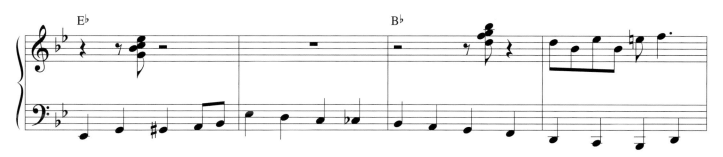

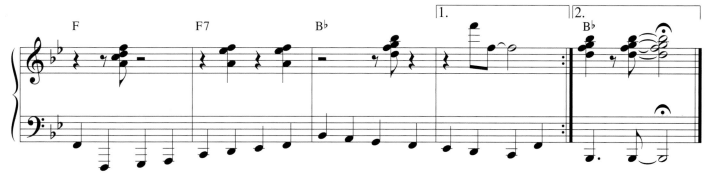

169 **New Note Warm-Up**

170 **Wade in the Water** CD :79

African-American Spiritual, U.S.A.

171 ***It Don't Mean a Thing
(If It Ain't Got That Swing)***

Words and Music by
DUKE ELLINGTON and IRVING MILLS

172 **Satin Doll** CD :80

Music by DUKE ELLINGTON

Band @ Home

LESSON 1

1. Practice "Duke's Place" with the accompaniment track.

LESSON 2

1. Practice "Wade in the Water" and "It Don't Mean a Thing (If It Ain't Got That Swing)."

LESSON 3

1. Practice "Satin Doll."

2. Improvise your own four-measure song using the notes concert F, E♭, and D. Be prepared to perform your improvisation for the class at our next meeting. Use the provided accompaniment track on your student CD. CD :81

Creative Tools of Music

Half Step—the distance between two adjacent notes

Interval—the distance between two pitches

Scale—a stepwise progression used in melodies and harmonies

Whole step—a musical distance that equals two half steps

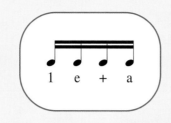

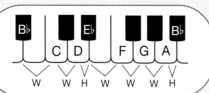

	W	W	H	W	W	W	H	
	1	2	3	4	5	6	7	8
Concert Key	B♭	C	D	E♭	F	G	A	B♭
C Instruments	B♭	C	D	E♭	F	G	A	B♭
B♭ Instruments	C	D	E	F	G	A	B	C
E♭ Instruments	G	A	B	C	D	E	F♯	G
F Instruments	F	G	A	B♭	C	D	E	F

173 *There Are Many Flags in Many Lands*

Traditional, U.S.A.

Flowing

174 *Oranges and Lemons*

Folk Song, England

175 **Tinga Layo**

Folk Song, Jamaica

Calypso

176 **Concert B♭ Scale Warm-Up**

177 **Chester**

WILLIAM BILLINGS, U.S.A.

UNIT 28

178 **Peep Squirrel** CD :83

Folk Song, Africa

Mysterious

179 **Hao Peng You**

Folk Song, China

Flowing

180 **Kookabura**

Folk Song, Australia

181 *Ciranda* CD :84

Folk Song, Brazil

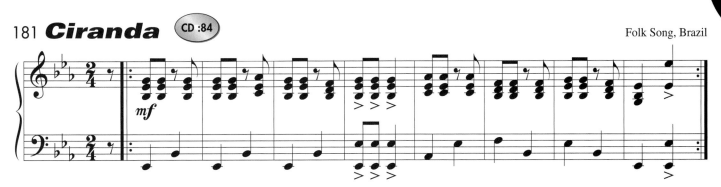

182 *Over the Rainbow*

Music by HAROLD ARLEN
Lyric by E.Y. HARBURG

Lyrical

183 *Creative Expression*

Band @ Home

LESSON 1

1. Practice "Oranges and Lemons" and "Tinga Layo." Perform them for your family and/or friends.

LESSON 2

1. Practice "Peep Squirrel."

2. Practice and memorize the concert B♭ scale.

LESSON 3

1. Count and play "Kookaburra" and "Over the Rainbow." Some students will have the chance to perform "Over the Rainbow" as a solo in the next band class.

2. On the line provided (183), create your own eight measure composition, using the key indicated and the rhythms you have learned so far.

Key of C

184 *Lip Slurs*

Moderato

185 *On the High "C's"*

186 *Wabash Cannonball*

Traditional, U.S.A.

187 **Matchmaker** CD :85

Lyrics by SHELDON HARNICK
Music by JERRY BOCK

Allegro

188 **Sleeping Beauty**

PETER ILYICH TCHAIKOVSKY, Russia

Allegro

189 *"B" Your Best*

190 **Theme From Ice Castles (Through the Eyes of Love)** CD :86

Music by MARVIN HAMLISCH
Lyrics by CAROLE BAYER SAGER

191 *Concert C Major Scale*

192 *Santa Lucia*

Moderato

Folk Song, Italy

mf

193 *Doo Wah Diddy Diddy* CD :87

Words and Music by
JEFF BARRY and ELLIE GREENWICH

Moderato

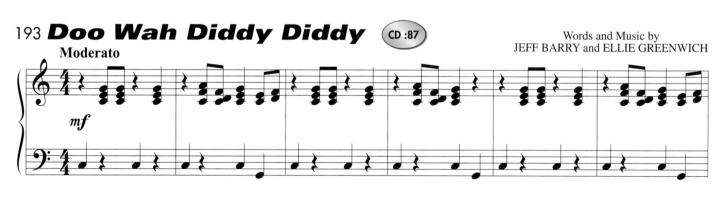

mf

f

UNIT 28

194 **The Hey Song** CD :88

By MIKE LEANDER and GARY GLITTER

This Arrangement © 2003 Palan Music Publishing Ltd. and Songs of Universal, Inc. All Rights Reserved

Band @ Home

LESSON 1

1. Practice "Wabash Cannonball" and "Matchmaker, Matchmaker."

2. Ask your family and friends the name of the Broadway musical in which "Matchmaker, Matchmaker" was performed. ("Fiddler on the Roof")

LESSON 2

1. Perform "Theme from Ice Castles (Through the Eyes of Love)" for your family and friends. Ask if anyone has heard this song before and if so where.

LESSON 3

1. Perform "The Hey Song" in the new key for your family and friends.

2. On Worksheet #1, compose an 8-measure warm-up. You will have the chance to play this in class. This should contain some of the things we have discussed before that are contained in a good warm-up.

93

PORTRAIT

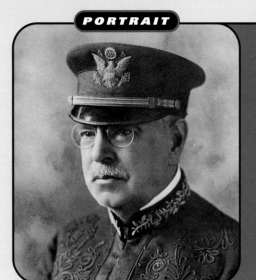

John Philip Sousa
(1854–1932)

Sometimes known as the "March King," John Philip Sousa wrote some of the most famous and recognizable marches in the world. Sousa was born in 1854 and he started studying music at the age of 6. When he was 13 years old his father enlisted Sousa in the Marines after he tried to run away from home to play in a circus band. In 1880, Sousa was appointed conductor of the United States Marine Band in Washington DC, which is known as "The President's Own." He later organized the Sousa Band and traveled the country presenting concerts with this organization. Throughout his illustrious career, Sousa wrote over 130 marches. In 1987, his "Stars and Stripes Forever" became the official march of the United States of America.

195 *More Lip Slurs*

196 *Caissons Go Rolling Along* CD :89

EDMUND L. GRUBER

197 Marines Hymn

Traditional, U.S.A.

198 Anchors Aweigh CD :90

Words and Music by
Capt. ALFRED H. MILES, U.S.N. (Ret.) and CHAS. A. ZIMMERMANN

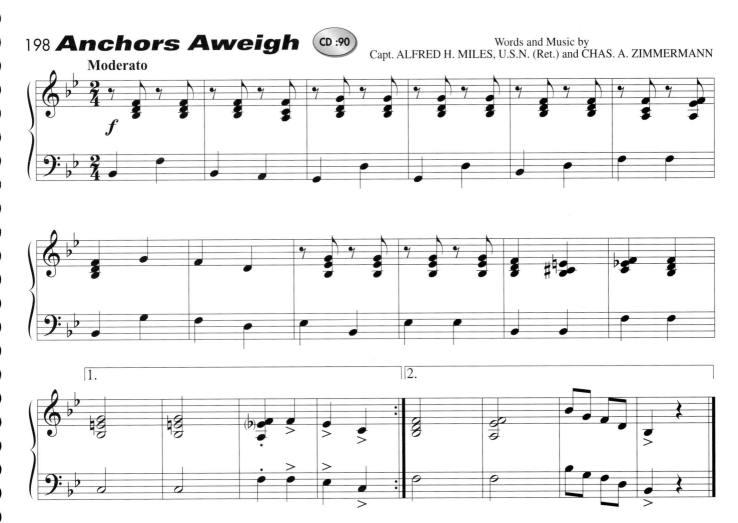

199 *El Capitan*

JOHN PHILIP SOUSA, U.S.A.

200 *The Thunderer*

JOHN PHILIP SOUSA, U.S.A.

201 *Blow Away the Morning Dew*

Folk Song, England

202 *The Yellow Rose of Texas* CD :91

Traditional, U.S.A.

Moderato

203 **Na Na Hey Hey** CD :92

(Kiss Him Goodbye)

Words and Music by
GARY DE CARLO, DALE FRASHUER and PAUL LEKA

Allegro

Band @ Home

LESSON 1

1. Practice "Caissons Go Rolling Along," "The Marines Hymn," and "Anchors Aweigh."

2. Ask your family members if they can identify which branch of the U.S. Armed Services these marches represent.

LESSON 2

1. Teach your family and friends about the composer John Philip Sousa.

2. Play "El Capitan" and "The Thunderer" for your family and friends.

LESSON 3

1. Practice "Blow Away the Morning Dew," "The Yellow Rose of Texas," and "Na Na Hey Hey (Kiss Him Goodbye)."

2. As you practice these three pieces, remember to play with the best sound possible, with the correct note values, and with the proper articulations.

Johann Sebastian Bach
(1685–1750)

Johann Sebastian Bach was one of the most important composers in European history. He was a church musician all of his life and people today still regularly sing and play his music in church. He did not play the piano until he was an old man, so most of his keyboard music was composed for the organ or clavichord, a very popular keyboard instrument during the Baroque era. The Baroque era style included much ornamentation that was added to clothing, furniture, and architecture. Baroque music also was very ornamented.

204 *Down and Up*

Band
Expressions

205 **Manhattan Beach** CD :93

Moderate

JOHN PHILIP SOUSA, U.S.A.
Arranged by MICHAEL STORY

(continued on page 100)

(Manhattan Beach, continued from page 99)

206 *Arirang* **CD :94**

Folk Song, Korea
Arranged by MICHAEL STORY

207 ***Expressions in Blue*** CD :95

ROBERT W. SMITH

Expressions in Blue - 2

208 *Bach Chorale*

JOHANN SEBASTIAN BACH, Germany
Arranged by ROBERT W. SMITH

209 **Let Freedom Ring** CD :96

Traditional
Arranged by ROBERT W. SMITH

Eine Kleine Nachtmusik

WOLFGANG AMADEUS MOZART, Austria

Eine Kleine Nachtmusik

WOLFGANG AMADEUS MOZART, Austria

Music for the Royal Fireworks

GEORGE FRIDERIC HANDEL, Germany/England
Arranged by SANDRA DACKOW

Moderato

Band @ Home

LESSON 1 & **LESSON 2**

1. Review all of our concert pieces we have played so far.

2. Remember to isolate the more difficult passages, playing them slowly before gradually increasing the speed.

3. Make a recording of your performance of each piece and turn it in at our next lesson. Write down what you discovered from critically listening to yourself play. Your teacher will review your recording and provide feedback for improvement.

UNITS 33–36
ARE PRESENTED BY YOUR TEACHER

Quarter 1

Quarter 2

Quarter 3

Quarter 4

Treasury of Scales: Concert B♭

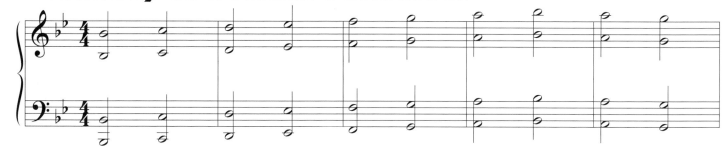

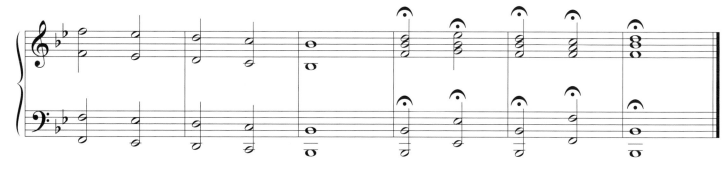

Treasury of Scales: Concert E♭

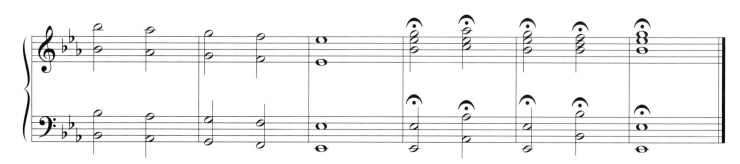

Treasury of Scales: Concert F

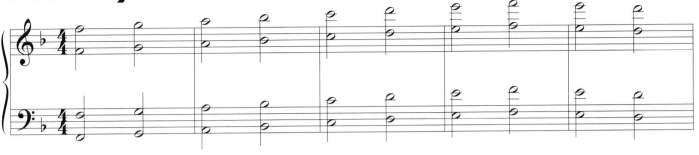

Treasury of Scales: Concert C

Glossary

Page numbers refer to the Student Book page where the definition is shown.

1st and 2nd Endings—*Play the 1st ending, repeat the section and play only the 2nd ending the second time.* (18)

Accent—*Play the note with more emphasis.* (18)

♯, ♭, ♮ **Accidental**—*A sharp, flat, or natural not indicated in the key signature.* (20)

Allegro—*Fast tempo.* (26)

Anacrusis—*One or more notes that come before the first full measure.* (14)

Andante—*Moderately slow (walking) tempo.* (26)

Articulation—*A slight interruption of the air stream with the tongue.* (4)

Balance—*All parts played and heard equally. The dynamic strength and importance given to instruments/voices within a composition.* (10)

Bar Line—*The vertical line placed on a staff to divide the music into measures.* (4)

❜ **Breath Mark**—*A recommended place to breathe.* (4)

Canon—*Music in which the melody is introduced in one voice and echoed by another voice.* (8)

Carol—*A song of praise or celebration.* (–)

Chorale—*A slow, "hymn-like" composition.* (12)

Chord—*Three or more tones sounded at the same time.* (18)

Clef—*A symbol placed at the beginning of the staff to identify the note names on the staff.* (4)

Common Time—*4/4 time signature.* (–)

Crescendo, Cresc.—*Gradually get louder.* (34)

Da Capo, D.C.—*Return to the beginning.* (36)

D.S.—**Dal Segno**—*Repeat from the sign.* (40)

Decrescendo, Decresc.—*Gradually get softer.* (34)

Dot—*Increases the value of the preceding note or rest by one half.* (18)

Duet—*A piece of music with two interacting parts.* (10)

Dynamics—*Musical performance levels of loud and soft.* (14)

Embouchure—*The natural formation of the facial and lip muscles on the mouthpiece or reeds.* (4)

⌢ **Fermata**—*Hold the note or rest longer than note value.* (4)

Final Bar Line—*Placed on the staff to indicate the end of a piece of music.* (4)

Fine—*The end.* (36)

♭ **Flat**—*A symbol that lowers the pitch of a note one half step.* (4)

Folk Song—*A song of cultural heritage passed from generation to generation sometimes through aural tradition.* (–)

𝆑 **Forte**—*Loud.* (14)

Grand Staff—*The Treble and Bass Clef staves joined together.* (4)

Half Step—*The distance between two adjacent notes.* (42)

Harmony—*The result of two or more tones sounded at the same time.* (10)

Improvisation—*Spontaneously creates a new melody without the intent to revise.* (40)

Interval—*The distance between two pitches.* (4)

Intonation—*The accuracy of pitch or pitch relationships in the performance of music.* (6)

Introduction—*A short section of music at the beginning of a piece.* (20)

Jazz—*Music rooted in improvisation and characterized by syncopated rhythms.* (40)

Key—*The tonality of a piece of music.* (10)

Key Signature—*Flats and sharps placed immediately following the clef used to indicate which notes are to be altered throughout the piece.* (10)

Largo—*A very slow tempo.* (34)

Ledger Lines—*Short lines placed above or below the staff for pitches beyond the range of the staff.* (4)

Legato—*Smooth and connected without interruption between the notes.* (32)

March—*Music for a parade or procession.* (10)

Measure—*The space between two bar lines to form a grouping of beats.* (4)

𝄎 **Measure Repeat sign**—*A symbol that indicates to repeat the previous measure.* (30)

Melody—*A series of musical tones that form a recognizable phrase to express a composer's thoughts or statements.* (16)

𝑚𝑓 **Mezzo Forte**—*Medium loud.* (14)

Glossary *continued*

mp **Mezzo Piano**—*Medium soft.* (14)

Moderato—*Moderate or medium tempo.* (26)

Multiple Measure Rest—*A symbol indicating more than one measure of rest.* (22)

Music Alphabet—*Letter names of the notes used in music.* (4)

Musical Line—*Direction or shape of a musical thought or idea.* (10)

♮ **Natural**—*A symbol which cancels a previous sharp or flat. Like a flat or sharp, it is used for the entire measure.* (20)

Ostinato—*A repeated melodic or rhythmic pattern.* (16)

Phrase—*A musical sentence or statement.* (12)

p **Piano**—*Soft.* (14)

Rehearsal Numbers/Letters—*Markings above the staff that indicate specific locations in the music.* (22)

Repeat Sign—*Symbol that indicates to go back and play the section of music again.* (12)

‖: *Repeat from the beginning*

:‖ *Repeat of a section*

Rest—*A silent unit of time.* (6)

Rhythm—*The organization of sound and silence in time.* (4)

Ritardando, Rit.—*Gradually slowing down.* (38)

Rock—*A style of popular music which originated in America characterized by a strong rhythmic beat and electronic instruments.* (20)

Roll—*An even sustained sound on a percussion instrument.* (–)

Roll Base—*The rhythmic pattern that serves as the foundation for each roll stroke.* (–)

Rubric—*A scoring procedure that indicates different levels of achievement.* (–)

Scale—*A series of tones arranged in a set pattern from low to high or high to low forming a stepwise progression used in melodies and harmonies.* (42)

♯ **Sharp**—*A symbol that raises the pitch of a note one half step.* (4)

Sight-reading—*Reading and performing a piece of music for the first time.* (14)

Slur—*A curved line placed above or below two or more different pitches to indicate that they are to be performed smoothly and connected.* (16)

Soli—*A line of music played by a small group of instruments.* (6)

Solo—*A performance by one person playing alone, with or without accompaniment.* (8)

Staccato—*Play the note lightly and detached.* (32)

Staff—*5 lines and 4 spaces on which notes and other musical symbols are placed.* (4)

Style—*The way in which music is expressed or performed.* (22)

Subdivide—*Dividing a note into smaller sections or fractions.* (14)

Swing—*A style of jazz music characterized by the "lengthening" of the eighth notes that are on the beat.* (40)

Syncopation—*Rhythm with the emphasis or stress on a weak beat or weak portion of a beat.* (38)

Tempo—*The speed of the beat.* (16)

Tenuto—*A symbol which means to play the note full value.* (32)

Tie—*A curved line connecting two notes of the same pitch and played as if they were one.* (16)

Time Signature—*A symbol placed at the beginning of the staff where the top number indicates the number of beats per measure and the bottom number what kind of note gets one beat.* (4)

Tutti—*All play* (6).

Unison—*All performers sound the same note.* (10)

Whole step—*A musical distance that equals two half steps.* (42)